AU

ALRA
www.alra.co.uk

Also by Julian Mitchell
in the Amber Lane Plays series

After Aida
Another Country
Falling Over England
Francis

AUGUST

An adaptation of Chekhov's
UNCLE VANYA
by
JULIAN MITCHELL
from a translation by Tania Alexander

AMBER LANE PRESS

All rights whatsoever in this play are strictly reserved and application for performance, etc. must be made before rehearsals begin to:

Peters, Fraser & Dunlop Ltd
5th Floor, The Chambers,
Chelsea Harbour,
London SW10 0XF

No performance may be given unless a licence has been obtained.

First published in 1994 by
Amber Lane Press Ltd,
Cheorl House, Church Street,
Charlbury, Oxford OX7 3PR
Telephone: 0608 810024

Printed in Great Britain by
Bocardo Press, Didcot, Oxon.

English version copyright © Julian Mitchell, 1994

The right of Julian Mitchell to be identified as author of this work has been asserted by him in accordance with Section 77 of the Copyright, Designs and Patents Act 1988.

ISBN 1 872868 14 2

Introduction

AUGUST is a version of Anton Chekhov's *Uncle Vanya*. The play began life as *The Wood Demon*, written in 1889. Performed in Moscow that December, it was poorly received, and though it was published the following year, Chekhov refused to allow any further productions. No one knows exactly when he rewrote it, but *Uncle Vanya*, which has many of the same characters and some identical speeches, was published with *The Seagull* in 1897 and performed with success round the provincial Russian theatres. It was produced by the Moscow Art Theatre in October 1899.

I have loved Chekhov with a passion from the first play of his I saw forty years ago—it was *The Cherry Orchard* at the Lyric, Hammersmith, in John Gielgud's production, with Gwen Ffrangcon-Davies as Madame Ranevsky, Esmé Percy as Gayev and Trevor Howard as Lopakhin. But though I have seen many, many productions of the four great Chekhov masterpieces, I have always felt there was something preventing me getting to the very heart of them. I assumed this was to do with the inevitable losses of translation into English. Then I saw Thomas Kilroy's version of *The Seagull* set in Ireland and realised that what was getting in the way was the well-meaning attempt to be faithful to the Russian original.

In most British productions of Chekhov there are birch forests, wooden dachas, samovars. Although it is utterly confusing to British audiences, producers doggedly persist with the use of Russian patronymics. As a result the spectators spend the first twenty minutes turning the pages of their programmes and asking each other who is who. All this (by now very conventional) 'Russianness' comes as a curtain between us and the plays, making them seem more foreign than they really are.

Once translated to a culture we understand, the plays cease to be foreign. Having a teapot instead of a samovar, and people called Ieuan instead of Ivan Ivanovitch, clears away a lot of distraction. Birch forests are undoubtedly real and Russian, but to get the same sense they give of vast distances spreading to the east, we look west to the Atlantic Ocean. Our Vladivostok is Patagonia.

The intellectual climate of pre-revolutionary Russia, in which the Professor in *Uncle Vanya* has thrived, has no British equivalent, and it is very difficult for us to imagine why his ideas should ever have enthralled the other characters. (Chekhov gives no actual examples.) But we do know that in Wales, in the 1890s, education was prized so highly that anyone who went to university was treated with enormous reverence.

That reverence was not always good for the graduate's spiritual life, or for that of the community at large. The self-important professor has been a negative factor in Welsh intellectual life ever since. But you have only to read the autobiography of Henry Jones—a shoemaker's son, born in 1852 at Llangernyw in Denbighshire, who became Professor of Philosophy at Glasgow and devised the penny rate to help pay for higher education in Wales—to realise how profound the hunger and respect were for university education at that time. It is very easy to believe that a Welsh Vanya and Sonya—Ieuan and Sian in *August*—would genuinely have sat up all night reading their hero's books.

There are other elements of Welsh life in the 1890s which are highly appropriate to *Uncle Vanya*. The agricultural depression was such that large estates were having real difficulty in making ends meet. Landlords were obliged to reduce rents, to their own permanent detriment: it was the beginning of the end for many of the old gentry. Though there were no peasants as such, language divided the anglicised landlords from their tenants. Even the bankruptcy of 'Pocky' Prosser can be related to the failure of the ship-building industry in the ports of Merioneth and Caernarvonshire. And of course Chekhov was extraordinarily early in his appreciation of the green issues which so preoccupy us today—pollution, deforestation, the destruction of the environment.

Though Chekhov was not himself a believer, he portrayed religious people with great sympathy in both stories and plays. His Sonya, with her almost ecstatic vision, would have felt quite at home with the Welsh fervour of the 1890s. Her disapproval of alcohol chimes exactly with the Welsh temperance movement. Altogether the more you look, the more parallels there are to be found.

The object of this version is not, however, to find modern or Welsh equivalents for everything in the original, but to liberate the play from its false British 'Russianness' and allow it to speak to us directly. A play is not about its setting, but its characters, and these remain true to themselves, and true to nature, wherever you put them.

I have made the Davieses old Welsh squires, thoroughly anglicised, and with English educations. They speak English amongst themselves, but Ieuan converses with most of the tenants in Welsh, and Sian, largely brought up by Gwen, is equally at home in both languages. The same is true of Michael Lloyd, who has done his medical training in London. Blathwaite is completely English, as is his wife Helen: neither has any Welsh. Thomas Prosser comes from a less well-educated background. Gwen was born into a monoglot Welsh family on the estate.

The Davieses don't give a thought to their race or nationality: they are what they've always been. They are slightly decayed from the time when Ieuan's father was an MP, partly because of Ieuan's temperament, partly because of the general agricultural depression of the 1880s and 1890s.

Professor Blathwaite and his wife are not only townspeople who feel ill at ease in the country but English who patronise the Welsh by instinct.

Of all the great critical blunders in history, none surpasses Tolstoy's remark to Chekhov after seeing *Uncle Vanya*: 'You know I can't stand Shakespeare, but your plays are even worse than his.'

From all the people who have helped me with this version, I should like particularly to thank Tania Alexander, who did the translation from which I worked, and who has been a guide, philosopher and friend throughout; and Huw Roberts, who has been an endless source of information on North Welsh life in the 1890s, and without whom the characters would have been disgracefully monoglot.

                                           Julian Mitchell
                                           Llansoy, 1994

Cast

Alexander Blathwaite, a retired professor
Helen, his wife, aged 27
Sian, his daughter by his first wife
Mair Davies, the widow of an MP, and mother of Blathwaite's first wife
Ieuan Davies, her son, aged 47
Michael Lloyd, a doctor
Thomas 'Pocky' Prosser, an impoverished local ship-builder
Gwen, an old Nanny
Roberts, a gamekeeper
A Workman
A Servant

The action takes place outside and inside the very large house at the centre of the Davies' estate, in the 1890s.

August was first presented at Theatr Clwyd, Mold on 25th October 1994. It was directed by Anthony Hopkins with the following cast:

MICHAEL LLOYD ...... Gawn Grainger
IEUAN DAVIES ...... Anthony Hopkins
A WORKMAN ...... Rhodri Hugh
MAIR DAVIES ...... Rhoda Lewis
POCKY PROSSER ...... Hugh Lloyd
SIAN ...... Rhian Morgan
HELEN ...... Lisa Orgolini
ALEXANDER BLATHWAITE ...... Leslie Phillips
GWEN ...... Menna Trussler

Set Designer: Eileen Diss
Costume Designer: Dani Everett
Lighting Designer: Nick Beadle

Act One

The terrace of a house in Caernarvonshire.

A heavy summer afternoon. In the distance the slow sound of the sea on a long sandy shore.

Under an old poplar in the avenue, a table is set for tea. There are garden seats and chairs. A swing hangs from a tree.

GWEN, the heavy, slow-moving, elderly Nanny, is sitting at the tea table, knitting a sock.

MICHAEL LLOYD, the local doctor, is pacing up and down. He has a huge moustache.

GWEN looks up from her knitting.

GWEN   What you want is a nice cup of tea.

   [*She starts to lift the teapot.*]

LLOYD   I don't feel like tea.

GWEN   No! Whisky, that's what you're feeling like ... And Robert Jones, Llanbedr, your own great uncle, a founder of the Band of Hope ...

   [*LLOYD is slightly hurt.*]

LLOYD   I don't drink every day, you know. Anyway, it's too hot. [*broods a moment*] How long have you known me, Gwenny?

GWEN   [*reflects*] O'r Annwyl, let me see—when did Dr Lloyd first come here? Sian's Mam was still alive, I know that, because you came to see her those last two winters, didn't you? And she died nine years ago, so—eleven years. Must be eleven years. Could be more, mind.

LLOYD   And haven't I changed!

GWEN   O'r Achold fawr, ay! You were a handsome young man in those days. Now—well, you're older. And not so good-looking. And you drink whisky.

LLOYD   Yes, but why, Gwenny?

GWEN   Well, if you ask me, it all began with your mother. If she'd stayed Chapel, instead of marrying a churchman ...

LLOYD   No, no ... Why have ten years made me such a different man?

        [GWEN *hardly seems to understand the question.*]

Because I'm overworked. On my feet from morning till night, never a moment to myself. And then, when I do get to bed, I don't sleep properly, because I'm always expecting to be dragged out to some wretched patient. I haven't had a single day off all the time you've known me. Of course I look older. Country life's so boring, so stupid, so squalid —it really gets me down. So many eccentrics, so many 'characters'. After a couple of years in the sticks, you become a 'character' yourself. You can't help it. You don't even notice. Look at this ridiculous moustache ... I've become a 'character', Gwenny. Not a stupid one, please God. Not yet. I can still think a bit. But as to feeling ... There's nothing I want, nothing I need, nothing I love.

        [*He kisses the top of* GWEN's *head.*]

Except you, perhaps. I love you. You're just like my Nanny when I was a boy.

GWEN   Why don't you have something to eat?

LLOYD   No thanks. Last February, you know, I had to go to Blaenau—help with the typhoid epidemic. Rows of people lying on the floors in their damp tubercular cottages. Filth, stench, smoke, babies, cats and dogs ... I worked all day, never sat down, not a moment to eat. And I couldn't relax even when I got home. They'd brought the signalman from Llandecwyn. Emergency. Had to operate at once. Well, I got him on the table, gave him the chloroform—and he went and died on me before I could even lift the knife. And then—it was the last thing I wanted, Gwen—my feelings—I suddenly felt... My conscience woke up. As though I'd deliberately killed the man. And I sat down. I closed my eyes—just like this. And I thought, the people who live a hundred, two hundred years from now, the people for whom we're paving the way—will they remember us? Will they spare us a single kind thought? I don't think so.

GWEN They may not remember, but God will.

LLOYD Thank you, Gwenny. That's well said. Thank you.

[IEUAN DAVIES *comes out of the house. He has been having a nap after lunch and looks dishevelled. He sits on a bench and adjusts his fashionable tie.*]

IEUAN Yes... [*Pause.*] Yes...

LLOYD Nice nap?

IEUAN Very. Very. [*yawns*] Ever since the Herr Professor and Mrs Blathwaite came to live here, life's been completely upside down. I sleep at the wrong time. I eat the wrong kind of food. I drink... It's very unhealthy. Before, I never had a moment to myself. Sian and I, we worked round the clock, and were perfectly happy. But now, she does all the work, and I just sleep, eat and drink. It's disgraceful.

GWEN [*shaking her head*] Popeth yn bendramwnwgl —higgledy-piggledy! Breakfast at eight, but the professor doesn't get up till twelve. Dinner these days—we used to have it at one o'clock, like everyone else, but now—he wants it at six! Then he sits up all night, reading and writing, till two in the morning, then—Gwarchod pawb! There goes his bell... What is it, what is it? What does he want? Tea! He wants tea! And people have to be woken up to put the kettle on, and... Duw a'n helpo! Popeth yn bendramwnwgl!

LLOYD   How much longer are they staying?

IEUAN   [*whistles*] Till the end of time. He's decided to live here.

GWEN   Look at this tea by here. Stone cold. And stewing for two hours while they decide to take a walk.

IEUAN   Never mind, here they are, here they are.

          [*Voices can be heard from the bottom of the garden as* ALEXANDER BLATHWAITE, *his wife* HELEN, *his daughter* SIAN *and* THOMAS PROSSER (*known as 'Pocky' because of his pockmarked face*) *return from their walk.* BLATHWAITE *is wearing an overcoat and galoshes, and carries an umbrella and gloves.*]

BLATHWAITE   Beautiful—beautiful. Very picturesque.

PROSSER   Picturesque, Professor, yes, that's just the word. Picturesque.

SIAN   We'll go to the new plantation tomorrow. You'd like that, Dada, wouldn't you?

IEUAN   Tea, ladies and gentlemen! Teatime!

BLATHWAITE   Oh—send mine to my study, would you? I want to make a couple of notes while the landscape's still fresh in my mind.

SIAN   You'll really love the walk to the plantation. You can see Snowdon.

          [HELEN, BLATHWAITE *and* SIAN *go into the house.* PROSSER *goes and sits next to* GWEN *and mops his brow.*]

IEUAN   Yes, quite. It's very hot, very close, but the great metropolitan thinker wears an overcoat and galoshes, and carries an umbrella and gloves.

LLOYD   Obviously believes in looking after himself.

IEUAN   But isn't she lovely? Isn't she beautiful? Have you ever seen a more beautiful woman in your life?

PROSSER   You know, Gwenny, it doesn't matter what I'm doing—driving my trap along the lane, walking in the garden, just looking at this table—I feel so happy. The weather's fine, the birds are singing, you can hear the sea—we're all good friends—what more could anyone ask?

[GWEN *gives him a cup of tea.*]

Diolch. Diolch yn fawr.

IEUAN   Those eyes... She's so—so...

LLOYD   All right, Ieuan...

IEUAN   What?

LLOYD   Tell me what's been happening.

IEUAN   Here? Nothing. Everything just as it always was. Look at me. Same as ever, only worse, because I'm so lazy now, I do nothing at all. Except grumble about like an old woman. As for Mother, she burbles on about the rights of women, as she always has, one eye on the grave, the other squinting hopefully into learned articles for the dawn of a new life.

LLOYD   And Professor Blathwaite?

IEUAN   Oh, the Herr Professor sits in his study, penning great thoughts far into the night. 'With furrowed brow and tortured brain, Our mighty intellect we strain, The search for insight all in vain.' Scribble, scribble, scribble—makes you sorry for the paper. He ought to write his autobiography—such a good subject. A retired professor, a sort of shrivelled academic dinosaur—riddled with gout and rheumatism and migraine—his liver swollen with jealousy and envy—this poor English professor is forced to live on his first wife's Welsh property because he can't afford to live in London. And complains day and night about how unfortunate he is, though he's really very lucky. [*He becomes excited.*] Incredibly lucky! He's only the son of some suburban London clerk, but he gets to university, studies metaphysics, is given a chair, marries the daughter of a Member of Parliament—it's one triumph after another. And that's not the half of it. He's been lecturing and writing about art for twenty-five years and never understood the first thing about it. For twenty-five years he's been masticating other people's thoughts on realism, naturalism, God-knows-what-ism. For twenty-five years he's been drivelling on about things intelligent people have always known, and stupid ones don't care about anyway. For a quarter of a century he's been wasting his and everyone else's time pouring this drivel from one empty vessel into another. And the conceit! The pretension! Only now he's retired, and not one person in the entire world has ever heard of him. He's totally unknown. Which means that for twenty-five years he's been holding down a job which someone else should have had. But there he goes, strutting about like God's gift to mankind.

LLOYD Oh, I see. You envy him.

IEUAN Of course I do. Look at the success he has with women. Don Juan wasn't a patch on the Herr Professor. First my sister, Hannah, wife number one—lovely, gentle creature, pure as the driven snow, noble in feeling, generous in spirit—Hannah, you know, had more admirers than he ever had pupils, but she loved him as only the innocent can love, as though he were as pure-hearted and perfect as she was herself. Then there's my mother—still adores him, still inspired by a sort of holy terror of him. Then Helen, wife number two—beautiful, intelligent—well, you've just seen her. He was already an old man when she married him. But she's given him her youth, her beauty, her freedom, her scintillating ... How the hell does he do it?

LLOYD   She's faithful to him?

IEUAN   Deplorably.

LLOYD   Why so?

IEUAN   Because fidelity like that is false from start to finish. It's all lofty sentiment and no common sense. To be unfaithful to an old man you can't stand, that's unthinkable, immoral, oh dear me, yes. But to stifle your youth, kill all real feeling in your heart—that's not immoral, no, no, of course not.

[PROSSER *has become increasingly upset.*]

PROSSER   [*tearful*] Ieuan, I do wish you wouldn't talk like that. Really. Someone who betrays his wife or her husband is completely unreliable. The sort of person who'd betray his country too.

IEUAN   [*annoyed*] Shut up, Pocky.

PROSSER   I'm sorry. But my wife ran off with her lover the day after our wedding—because she couldn't bear my looks, she said, and ... But I've still not been unfaithful. I loved her then and I love her now and I help her all I can. Of course, I've not had much since the shipyard went under, but I've spent what I've had to give her children a proper English education. I've given up my happiness for her. But—I've still got my pride. While she—what's she got? She's lost her youth, her beauty, inevitably, has faded, her lover's died ...

[SIAN *and* HELEN *come on, followed by* MAIR

DAVIES, IEUAN's *mother.* MAIR *is reading a book and sits down without looking up from it. A cup of tea is put beside her which she drinks, still without looking up from the page.*]

SIAN [*to* GWEN] Gwenny, cariad, ma' rhai o blant y pentre wrth y drws. Ewch atyn nhw, ewch chi? Ofala i am y te. [*to* HELEN, *as she pours the tea*] It's the village children, Helen. They're always wanting something. Gwenny'll see to it.

[HELEN *takes a cup of tea over to the swing.* LLOYD *goes to her.*]

LLOYD Your note said your husband was very ill, Mrs Blathwaite. Rheumatism and you didn't know what. But he looks all right to me.

HELEN Well, he's all right today, but last night he was so depressed—he had these pains in his leg, you see.

LLOYD But I've come fifteen miles! Not for the first time either.

[HELEN *shrugs.*]

Well, never mind. Now I'm here I'll stay. Get a decent night's sleep for once.

SIAN Oh, good. You hardly ever stay the night. You haven't had dinner yet, have you?

LLOYD No.

SIAN Then you'll dine with us. We eat between six and seven now. [*drinks some tea*] This is cold!

PROSSER The temperature in the teapot does indeed appear to have dropped somewhat.

[GWEN *gets up and leaves, carrying the teapot.*]

HELEN It doesn't matter, Mr Prichard. It's nice, cold tea.

PROSSER Beg your pardon, madam, not Prichard, Prosser. Thomas Prosser. Pocky, some people call me, because of the marks on my face. Sian's godfather. Your husband, Professor Blathwaite, knows me well. I live here, madam, on the estate. Used to have a ship-building business, down in Pwllheli, but what with the railways, and... You may have been good enough to notice I dine with you every day.

SIAN   Mr Prosser's our right-hand man—helps us with everything. [*tenderly, to* PROSSER] Let me give my dear old godfather some more tea.

MAIR   [*out of nowhere*] Ah!

SIAN   Yes, Granny?

MAIR   I forgot to tell Alexander. My mind must be going. I had a letter from Henry Jones in Glasgow. He sent his new article.

LLOYD Interesting?

MAIR   Very. Though a little odd, I thought. He seems to be attacking the position I understood him to be defending seven years ago. Which is dreadful.

IEUAN Nothing dreadful about it, Mother. Drink your tea and shut up.

MAIR   But I want to talk.

IEUAN We've been talking and talking and reading pamphlets for fifty years. It's time we stopped.

MAIR   Why shouldn't I talk if I want to? You've changed so much this last year, Ieuan, I hardly know you. You used to be a man of sound opinions, someone with truly enlightened views.

IEUAN Enlightened views! Which enlightened precisely who? Enlightened views! [*Pause.*] You couldn't have hurt me more if you'd tried. I'm forty-seven, Mother. And up to a year ago I tried, like you, to fuddle my brains with all that academic drivel. So I could escape seeing life as it really is. And I honestly thought I was doing the right thing. Now... If you only knew. I lie awake all night, cursing myself for having been so stupid, wasting

my time on 'views' when I could have been—could
have done ... And now I'm too old!

SIAN   Uncle, you're being tiresome again.

MAIR   [*to* IEUAN] There was nothing wrong with the ideas.
If you had beliefs and didn't act on them, that's
your fault. You should have done something about
them.

IEUAN What, turn myself into a scribbling machine like
your dear Herr Professor?

MAIR   And what's that supposed to mean?

SIAN   [*pleading*] Granny! Uncle! Please.

IEUAN All right. I apologise. Won't say another word.
       [*Pause.*]

HELEN It's such a lovely day today. Not too hot.
       [*Pause.*]

IEUAN Perfect day to hang yourself.
       [PROSSER *has taken out a mouth organ and is
       tuning up.* GWEN *appears in the garden, calling
       the hens.*]

GWEN   Chook, chook, chook, chook...

SIAN   Beth oedd ar y plant isie, Gwenny?

GWEN   Casglu at y Genhadaeth Dramor. Chook, chook,
chook...

SIAN   [*to* HELEN] The children were collecting for the
missionaries. [*to* GWEN] Am p'run 'dach chi'n
chwilio?

GWEN   Yr hen iar frech 'ne. Ma'i wedi crwydro i rywle efo'i
chywion bach. 'Berig i'r llwynogod 'u cael nhw.

SIAN   Lost the speckled hen again!
       [GWEN *leaves, still calling the hens.* PROSSER
       plays. Everyone listens in silence. LLOYD *goes
       over to* HELEN.]

LLOYD   If you'd like to look me up sometime—come over
        with Sian—I'd be delighted to show you my prop-
        erty. It's only small—ninety acres—but I've laid out
        the garden myself, if you're interested in that sort
        of thing. And there's an arboretum—nothing like it
        for a hundred miles. And next to my place there's a
        forestry plantation. The man in charge is old and ill,
        so I look after it, more or less.

HELEN   Someone said you were interested in trees. It's a
        very useful sort of work, of course. But for a
        doctor... Doesn't it get in the way of your true
        vocation?

LLOYD   Oh, God only knows what true vocations are.

HELEN   So you like trees?

LLOYD   Yes.

IEUAN   [ironical] Rather!

HELEN   [to LLOYD] But you're still so young. You can't be
        more than thirty-six, thirty-seven. And trees—
        they're not really that interesting, are they? A bit
        monotonous, surely?

SIAN   Not at all, Helen. Dr Lloyd plants new species
        every year. He's got a bronze medal, and a di-
        ploma, from the Welsh Agricultural Society. He's
        trying to stop the old woodlands being destroyed,
        you see. If you let him talk about it, you'll soon see
        how interesting it is.

                [She repeats her lesson.]

        Woods make the world more beautiful, they teach
        us to appreciate what beauty is, they inspire us with
        great thoughts. And they affect the climate. Here
        they make it mild. So Dr Lloyd can grow flowers
        you couldn't in parts of England. Also, in countries
        with a mild climate, man has less of a struggle with
        nature, so people are mild, too, more gentle.
        They're better-looking, more adaptable, more sen-

sitive, more intelligent. Their language is elegant, their movements graceful. Art and science flourish, philosophy is optimistic, and the attitude to women is genuinely refined and polite.

IEUAN Bravo! Bravo, Sian! Absolutely charming. Complete rot, of course. The people of Caernarvonshire are *not* better-looking, *not* more intelligent... [*to* LLOYD] Sorry, Michael, but I'm going to go on burning logs on *my* fire.

LLOYD Why not use peat? Why not build your barns of stone instead of wood? Of course you have to cut down trees when you really need them, but why destroy whole forests? The ship-builders at Port Madoc and Pwllheli, they used to get their timber from Maentwrog. Didn't they, Pocky?

PROSSER In the old days.

LLOYD But now, if they build ships at all, they use timber from the Baltic. Because Maentwrog is finished. All over the world forests are going under the axe, trees are disappearing by the million, animals and birds are losing their natural habitats, rivers are drying up. We're destroying the most beautiful scenery for ever, because people can't be bothered to bend down to pick up their own firewood. [*to* HELEN] Don't you agree, Mrs Blathwaite? Only a mindless barbarian would burn so much beauty and destroy things he himself can never replace. Man was endowed with reason and imagination so he could increase what he's been given, but he doesn't create, he destroys. There's less and less forest, rivers and wildlife are disappearing, the climate's changing for the worse, and the land's getting poorer and uglier every day. [*to* IEUAN, *who is smiling ironically*] Yes, I know you think I'm exaggerating—and perhaps I am a bit obsessed. But when I walk through woods that I've saved from the axe, when I hear the rustling of young trees I've planted with my own hands, I know I have some small influence over the climate. And if, in a thousand years' time, mankind is happy, then perhaps I'll have had just a little to do with it. When I plant a tree, and watch it grow, and sway in the wind, I'm filled with pride and ...

[*A* WORKMAN *comes on.*]

WORKMAN Excuse me, please, is the doctor here? [*sees* LLOYD] Oh, Dr Lloyd, ges i'n anfon i'ch nol chi.

LLOYD Be' sy'n bod?

WORKMAN Mae 'ne ddyn wedi'i anafu yn y chwarel.

LLOYD Oh! Mi ddo' i rwan. [*to the others*] Sorry, got to go. Man injured at the quarry, damn it, just when I ...

[*He looks round for his hat.*]

SIAN What a shame. But you can come back for dinner afterwards.

LLOYD No, no. It'll be too late then—far too late.

[*The* WORKMAN *goes.* LLOYD *sings a snatch of song, looking for his hat.*]

There's a man in a play I saw with a big moustache and no brains. That's me to a T. Well—goodbye, everyone. Perhaps I'm just a crank after all. Goodbye!

[*He heads towards the house.* SIAN *takes his arm as he goes.*]

SIAN When shall we see you again?

LLOYD Oh, God, Sian, I don't know.

SIAN You won't wait another month, I hope?

[*They go into the house together.* MAIR *and* PROSSER *stay where they are as* HELEN *and* IEUAN *go to the verandah.*]

HELEN You're being impossible again, Ieuan. Upsetting

your mother, calling Alexander a scribbler. And you started another argument with him at breakfast. It's so childish.

IEUAN But I can't stand him.

HELEN That's just stupid. He's no different from anyone else. No worse than you are, anyway.

IEUAN If you could only see your face, Helen, watch your movements. You're too bored to live. Absolutely—too bored to live.

HELEN I'm bored with everyone blaming Alexander, and pitying me, yes. Oh, dear, the poor thing, married to that awful old husband. All your bogus sympathy. It's just like the doctor said—you all go on mindlessly destroying the forests, so there'll soon be nothing left on earth. And you're mindlessly destroying human beings too. It's thanks to people like you, there'll soon be no loyalty, no fidelity, no capacity for self-sacrifice left in the world. If a woman's not yours, you should treat her with indifference. But you can't because—the doctor's so right—because you all have such a fierce destructive force in you. You don't care about trees, birds, or women, you don't even care for each other.

IEUAN Spare me your analysis, please.

[*Pause.*]

HELEN Dr Lloyd has such a tired, sensitive face. An interesting face. Sian's attracted to him, obviously. In fact she's in love with him. I can quite see why. He's been here three times since we came, but I still haven't had a real talk with him, I'm so shy and—I haven't even been nice to him. He thought I was rude, just now. I think you and I are friends because we're both such tedious and boring people. So boring! Don't look at me like that, please, it's not amusing.

IEUAN How else can I look when I love you? You're my happiness, my life, my youth. I know there's no chance of having my feelings returned, but I don't ask for that, I don't ask for anything, just to look at you, hear your voice ...

HELEN Ssh. They'll hear you.

> [*She starts towards the house.*]

IEUAN [*following her*] Let me talk to you, let me tell you how much I love you, don't send me away. If I can just tell you how much ...

HELEN You're impossible!

> [*They go into the house.* PROSSER *plays his mouth organ.* MAIR *makes a note on her pamphlet.*]

End of Act One

Act Two

The dining room. Night.

A GAMEKEEPER *can be heard calling his dogs as he patrols the estate.*

BLATHWAITE *is sitting in an armchair by the open window, dozing.* HELEN *is sitting beside him, also dozing. There is a table covered with medicine bottles.*

BLATHWAITE *wakes with a start.*

BLATHWAITE Who's there? Sian? Is that you?

HELEN It's me.

BLATHWAITE Oh—Helen—the pain—it's unbearable.

HELEN Your rug's fallen off.

[*She picks it up and wraps it round his legs.*]

I'll close the window.

BLATHWAITE No, no, don't do that. It's stifling in here. I was asleep. I was dreaming my left leg didn't belong to me. Then I woke up with this agonising pain. It's not gout. More like rheumatism. What time is it?

HELEN Twenty past midnight.

[*Pause.*]

BLATHWAITE Look out Ruskin for me in the morning, would you? *Stones of Venice.* I'm sure we've got it.

HELEN What?

BLATHWAITE Ruskin. *Stones of Venice.* Find it for me in the morning. It's in the library somewhere. Why is it so hard for me to breathe?

HELEN You're tired. This is the second night running you haven't slept.

BLATHWAITE I'm afraid it is gout. You can get angina from gout. Old age is so disgusting. Utterly damnable! And if it disgusts me, the rest of you must find me revolting even to look at.

HELEN It's not our fault you're old.

BLATHWAITE But you do find me revolting. You above all.

[HELEN *moves away and sits some distance from him.*]

Of course, you're quite right. I'm not stupid, I do understand. You're young, healthy, and beautiful, you want some life, and I'm so old I'm practically a corpse. Of course I understand. It's ridiculous I'm still alive. But just contain yourself, you'll soon be free. I shan't drag on much longer.

HELEN Oh, do stop, for God's sake. I'm so tired.

BLATHWAITE Everyone's tired, everyone's bored, everyone's wasting his youth because of me. I'm the only one having a good time. Obviously.

HELEN Please. I'm worn out with it.

BLATHWAITE I've worn everyone out. Of course!

HELEN [*through tears*] It's unbearable! What do you want from me?

BLATHWAITE Nothing.

HELEN Then please stop it. Please!

BLATHWAITE I find it very odd. When Ieuan holds forth, or his old fool of a mother, no one complains, everyone listens politely. But I only have to open my mouth and at once everyone's bored. The very sound of my voice repels you all. Well, all right, so I am repulsive, a selfish, tyrannical old man. But hasn't an old man the right to be a little selfish? Hasn't he earned it? I ask you, Helen, haven't I the right to a peaceful old age, with a little attention from other people?

HELEN No one's disputing your rights.

> [*The window bangs in the wind.*]

The wind's getting up. Listen to the sea. I'll shut the window.

> [*She goes to the window.*]

It's going to rain.

> [*She closes it.*]

No one's disputing your rights.

> [*Pause. The* GAMEKEEPER *can be heard whistling his dogs.*]

BLATHWAITE I've devoted my entire life to scholarship. I've lived between the study and the lecture room, discussing ideas with respected colleagues. Now suddenly, for no reason, I find myself in this ghastly Welsh mausoleum, meeting stupid people all day long, forced to listen to their boring conversation ... I want to have some life too. I like success, fame, excitement. Wales—it's like being in exile. I spend my whole time longing for the past, furious when I hear of other people's successes, terrified of dying ... I can't bear it! I haven't the strength. And no one here can forgive me for being old.

HELEN If you'll just have a little patience ... In five or six years I'll be old myself.

> [SIAN *comes in.*]

SIAN Dada, you asked us specially to send for Dr Lloyd, and here he is, come all this way, and you refuse to see him. It's not very polite.

BLATHWAITE What use is Lloyd to me? Knows about as much about medicine as I do about astronomy.

SIAN We can hardly ask the entire medical establishment to come from London just for your gout.

BLATHWAITE He's a fool, an idealist. I won't speak to him.

SIAN   Well—up to you. I wash my hands of it.

[*She sits.*]

BLATHWAITE   What time is it now?

HELEN   After midnight.

BLATHWAITE   I'm suffocating. Sian—give me those drops. On the table there.

[SIAN *goes to the table.*]

SIAN   Here you are.

BLATHWAITE   [*angry*] No, no, not those! Why can't anyone do what I ask?

SIAN   Don't be so grumpy. Some people may find it amusing, but I don't, I think it's silly. And I haven't time for it. I've got to get up at dawn for the haymaking.

[IEUAN *comes in, wearing a dressing gown and carrying a candle. There is a flash of lightning.*]

IEUAN   Going to be a storm. See that? Helen, Sian—you can go to bed now. I've come to do my stint.

BLATHWAITE   What? No! Don't leave me with Ieuan, for God's sake. He'll talk me to death.

IEUAN   They've got to get some rest. This is the second night running they've had no sleep.

BLATHWAITE   Well, they can go to bed. But so can you. Thank you, Ieuan. But in the name of our old friendship, please don't argue. We'll talk some other time.

IEUAN   [*mocking*] Old friendship—very old!

SIAN   Be quiet, Uncle.

BLATHWAITE   [*to* HELEN] Darling, don't leave me with him. He'll kill me, talking.

IEUAN   This is all quite preposterous.

[GWEN *comes in, yawning.*]

SIAN   Gwenny, cariad, what are you doing up at this hour?

GWEN   He'll be wanting his tea. I can't go to bed in case he wants his tea.

[*She yawns hugely.*]

BLATHWAITE   Everyone's exhausted. Except me. I'm fresh as a daisy, of course.

[GWEN *goes over to him and rearranges his rug and pillows.*]

GWEN   How are you feeling, love? Hurting, is it? I'm just the same, I've got this niggling little pain in my legs, sort of buzzing, like. And you've had yours such a long time, haven't you? I remember Sian's mother, she used to be up all night, worrying over you, she loved you so much. [*Pause.*] Old people are just like children—need someone to make a fuss of you, don't you? But no one cares. [*kisses him*] Time for bed, 'y nghariad i. Come along, yr hen lanc. I'll make you a nice pot of tea, and a hot water bottle—then I'll say my prayers and put you in.

BLATHWAITE   [*touched*] Thank you, Gwen.

GWEN   Buzzes away in my legs, it does. Niggle, niggle, niggle. And Mrs Blathwaite used to get so upset she'd burst into tears. She did, Sian. You were just a silly little girl then, you didn't notice. Come along, love, come along.

[GWEN *leads* BLATHWAITE *off.* SIAN *goes with them.*]

HELEN   He's worn me out. I can hardly stand.

IEUAN   He's worn you out, I've worn myself out. Third night running I haven't slept a wink.

HELEN   What a miserable lot we are. Your mother despises everyone and everything except her pamphlets and her Professor. He's tetchy and doesn't trust me, and is afraid of you. Sian's angry with him and me—hasn't spoken to me for a fortnight. You loathe

	him and despise your mother. I'm jumpy myself —almost burst into tears twenty times today. We're a miserable lot.

IEUAN   Spare me your analyses, please.

HELEN   Ieuan, you're a clever, educated man. You know perfectly well that what's wrong with the world isn't the big things, people burning forests, but the little ones—hatred, anger, all this petty squabbling. So why do you complain the whole time instead of trying to get people to get along together?

IEUAN   Have to reconcile me to myself first. Darling...

     [*He tries to kiss her. She moves away.*]

HELEN   Stop it! Go away!

IEUAN   The rain'll stop soon. Nature will be refreshed. The earth will breathe gently again. The sea will calm. But I shan't calm, I shan't be refreshed. I'm haunted night and day by my own ghost. Obsessed with the thought that my life is over. I've no past to look back on—I've wasted my life on trivialities. And the present is meaningless and horrible. I offer you my life, my love ... What am I to do with them? Where am I to put them? My love is like a ray of sunlight at the bottom of a deep pit. And my life's the same. Wasted.

HELEN   When you talk about love—I'm sorry, I go completely blank. I've got nothing to say. [*turns to go*] Goodnight.

IEUAN   [*barring her way*] If you only knew what horror it gives me to think of another life, your life, being wasted like mine, and in the very same house. What are you waiting for? What stupid notion of morality is holding you back? Don't you realise—don't you see ...?

HELEN   [*looking at him closely*] Ieuan, you're drunk.

IEUAN   Possibly—possibly...

HELEN Where's Dr Lloyd?

IEUAN In there. He's staying the night. Possibly—
possibly... Anything's possible.

HELEN Why are you drinking again?

IEUAN Gives me the illusion I'm alive. Don't ask me to
stop, Helen, for God's sake.

HELEN You never used to drink. Or talk so much. Go to
bed. You're a bore.

IEUAN [*trying to kiss her hand*] Darling—angel...

HELEN [*sad*] Leave me alone. This is all so disgusting.

       [*She goes.*]

IEUAN Gone. [*Pause.*] Ten years ago I used to meet her at
my poor dear sister's. She was seventeen then, I
was thirty-seven. So why didn't I fall in love with
her? Ask her to marry me? It would all have been
possible then. She'd be my wife now, and... Yes!
We'd have been woken by the storm, she'd have
been frightened by the thunder... I'd have held her
in my arms and whispered 'Don't be afraid, I'm
here, Ieuan's here'. What a lovely happy dream...
[*laughs*] God, but I'm so confused... Why am I old?
Why doesn't she understand me? All those rhetori-
cal questions she asks, her lazy idea of morality,
her lazy, stupid ideas about the destruction of the
world—I hate all that. [*Pause.*] God, I've been
cheated. I've worshipped at the shrine of Blathwaite, a pitiful, gout-ridden invalid. I've worked like
a slave for him—Sian and I, we've squeezed every
penny out of this land, in spite of the depression, in
spite of the fact we've had to lower rents. We've
been as mean as the local farmers, checking the
fatstock prices, haggling over hay, going short
ourselves to scrape the pennies and halfpennies
together to send to him. I was so proud of him and
his scholarship. He was my whole life and soul.

Everything he wrote or said was the inspiration of a genius. And now—oh, God—now he's retired, I can see what his life amounts to. Nothing. Not a page will survive. He's completely unknown, and always will be. A bubble reputation. And I've been cheated —it's all so obvious now—I've been cheated like the Welsh have always been cheated by the English ...

> [LLOYD *comes in. He is wearing a jacket with no tie or waistcoat, and is a little tipsy. He is much more Welsh when drunk.* PROSSER *follows, with his mouth organ.*]

LLOYD   Play something, man.

PROSSER   But everyone's asleep.

LLOYD   Play, I said.

> [PROSSER *plays very softly.*]

You all alone? No ladies?

> [*He sings quietly, a Welsh song.*]

I was woken by the storm. Nice drop of rain. What time is it?

IEUAN   God knows.

LLOYD   I thought I heard Mrs Blathwaite.

IEUAN   She was here, yes.

LLOYD   Lovely woman. Oh, God ...

> [*He looks at the medicine bottles on the table.*]

Medicines. Prescriptions from every town in England. Harley Street. Bath. Cheltenham. He's bored every physician in the empire with his wretched gout. Do you think he is ill, or just having us on?

IEUAN   He's ill.

> [*Pause.*]

LLOYD   What's the matter with you, then? Don't tell me you're sorry for him.

IEUAN   Leave me alone.

LLOYD   Or could it just possibly be that you're in love with Mrs Herr Professor Blathwaite?

IEUAN   She's my friend.

LLOYD   Already?

IEUAN   What?

LLOYD   A woman can only become a man's friend by a logical progression: companion, mistress, friend.

IEUAN   What a very vulgar mind you have.

LLOYD   Vulgar? Yes, I am vulgar. But then I'm drunk. I usually only get drunk like this once a month. And when I'm drunk I'm extremely arrogant and rude. Can do anything, mind. Undertake the most difficult operation, perform it perfectly, in the farmhouse, on the kitchen table. And make the most far-reaching plans for the future. I'm not a 'character' then, I really believe I'm doing humanity a great service—oh, very great! I have my own view of the world, then, when all my friends, people like you, you strike me as nothing but—but tiny insects—tuberculous microbes... Play, Pocky!

PROSSER   Now, look, Doctor, I'd like to play, cross my heart, I would, but everyone's asleep.

LLOYD   Play, man!

[PROSSER *plays softly.*]

What we need is a drink. Let's see if there's any of that brandy left. Then as soon as it's light, we'll go over my place, right? My assistant, unqualified, he never says 'right', it's always 'orl right'. Like a bloody Englishman. 'Orl right', then?

[SIAN *comes in.*]

Oh, excuse me, madam. Not got me tie on.

[*He goes off, followed by* PROSSER.]

SIAN   Uncle Ieuan! You've been drinking with the doctor.
         What a pair of bright sparks you are. He's always
         been like that, of course, but there's no need for
         you to start. You're too old for it.

IEUAN   What's age got to do with it? When you have no life
         of your own, you live on fantasies. They're better
         than nothing.

SIAN   We've cut the hay, but it rains every day and it's all
         rotting in the fields—and you live on fantasies! I
         don't know—you seem to have given up running
         this place altogether. I have to do it all on my
         own—and I'm exhausted. [*alarmed*] Uncle, you're
         crying.

IEUAN   Crying? Nonsense. Rubbish. It's just—you looked
         at me then just like your dear mother used to. Sian,
         cariad ... [*kissing her*] My sister, my dear, darling
         Hannah—where is she now? If only she knew. If
         only she knew.

SIAN   Knew what, Uncle?

IEUAN   It's so painful—it's no good—nothing—later
         —nothing—I'll ...

         [*He goes off.* SIAN *knocks on the door.*]

SIAN   Dr Lloyd? Are you awake? May I have a word?

LLOYD   [*through the door*] Just coming.

         [*He appears, now with waistcoat and tie.*]

         What can I do for you, Sian?

SIAN   You may drink yourself as much as your conscience
         allows, but please, please, don't let Uncle Ieuan
         drink too. It's so bad for him.

LLOYD   Right. No more drink. Promise. [*Pause.*] I'll leave
         right away. Cross my heart. By the time they've got
         my mare harnessed, it'll be daylight, anyway.

SIAN   Oh, don't go now, it's still raining. Wait till morn-
         ing.

LLOYD   No, the storm's gone the other way, we've only caught the tail of it. So I'll be off. And please—don't call me in again to see your father. I tell him it's gout, he says it's rheumatism. I say, lie down, he says, I'll sit up. And tonight he wouldn't even speak to me.

SIAN   He's spoiled.

[She goes to the sideboard.]

Would you like something to eat?

LLOYD   Well, just a bite, perhaps.

SIAN   I like eating at night. And there's usually something in here. They say he had great success with the ladies in his time, and they spoiled him. Yes, here's some cheese, look, have some of this.

[They stand together at the sideboard, eating.]

LLOYD   I haven't eaten all day. Only drunk. Your father's a very awkward fellow, you know. *[helps himself to whisky]* May I? *[drinks it down]* There's just us, so—may I be frank? I don't think I could stick a month in this house. The atmosphere'd choke me. Your father's totally obsessed with his gout and his books, Ieuan with his depression, your grandmother ... and your stepmother ...

SIAN   What about her?

LLOYD   Everything about a human being should be beautiful—face, dress, heart, mind. And she is beautiful, no denying that. But all she ever does is eat, sleep, and drift about, bewitching us all with her beauty. Nothing else. She has no function, everything's done for her. Isn't it? But an idle life can never be a good life. *[Pause.]* Well—perhaps that's too harsh. I'm as fed up with things as your uncle. We're becoming a pair of old grumps.

SIAN   Are you fed up with things?

LLOYD　Well—I love life in general. But I can't bear life here in the country, ordinary life. I despise it from the bottom of my heart. As for my personal life—oh, God, there's nothing good about it. Nothing. You know when you're walking through a wood at night? And you see a light glimmering in the distance, and you stop worrying that it's dark and you're tired, you don't even notice the branches scratching your face, because ... I work harder than anyone in this county—you know I do—but things never go my way, and sometimes I feel so low... But then I have no light glimmering for me in the distance. I don't expect anything any more, not for myself, I don't like people ... It's a long time since I loved another human being.

SIAN　No one?

LLOYD　Well, I do feel a certain tenderness for Gwenny. For old times' sake. But the farmers are all too much the same, so mean-spirited and hypocritical, they live such narrow lives, and the squires—I just can't get on with them. They wear me down. All of them, all of my friends here, are so shallow-minded, shallow-hearted. They can't see beyond the end of their noses. They're stupid, in fact. And the ones who aren't so stupid, who have something to them, they're all hysterical, or morbidly introspective and self-analytical—they whine, they sneer, they're pathologically malicious. They look sideways at you and say, 'He's a psychopath', or 'He's a windbag'. And when they don't know what label to attach to me, they say—[Welsh accent]—'Strange man, the doctor, very strange!' I like the woods—that's 'strange'. I don't eat meat—very 'strange'. [own voice] There's no spontaneity, no sincerity, no openness to nature or people—nothing.

　　　　[He reaches for another drink.]

SIAN Please don't drink any more—please.

LLOYD Why not?

SIAN It doesn't suit you. You're such a fine man—your voice is so gentle—and—and you—more than anyone I know—you're beautiful. You don't want to be like other people, drinking and playing cards. So don't—please! You're always saying how people don't create things, only destroy what's been given them by God. So why do you destroy yourself? Don't—please don't—I beg you.

LLOYD [holding out his hand] All right. I'll never have another drink again.

SIAN Promise?

LLOYD Word of honour.

SIAN [taking his hand warmly] Thank you.

LLOYD Finished! Now I'm sober. Completely sober. And will remain so for the rest of my days. [looks at his watch] But as I was saying—my time is over and done with. I've grown old, worked too hard, become vulgar and insensitive. I couldn't form an attachment to another human being now. I don't love anyone—and I never shall. The only thing that still touches me is beauty. I'm not indifferent to that. For instance, if Mrs Blathwaite wanted to, I honestly believe she could turn my head—like that. But of course that wouldn't be love, not true love.

[He covers his eyes with his hands and shivers.]

SIAN What's the matter?

LLOYD Nothing. You know, last February, one of my patients died under chloroform...

SIAN It's time you forgot about that. [Pause.] Doctor—suppose I had a friend—or a younger sister, say—and you discovered that she—well, that she was in love with you—what would you do?

LLOYD [*shrugging his shoulders*] I don't know. Ignore it. Tell her I couldn't love her—sorry, I was very busy... Look, I'd better go if I'm going, or we'll stay here talking till dawn. Goodbye, Sian. [*shakes her hand*] I'll go through the sitting room, if that's all right, or your Uncle Ieuan'll catch me and I'll never get off at all.

       [*He goes.*]

SIAN He didn't say anything. And I've no idea what he really thinks or feels. So why do I feel so happy? [*laughs with happiness*] I told him—you're such a fine man, such a gentle voice, you're beautiful. Perhaps I shouldn't have said that. Yet his voice is so musical—I can still feel it vibrating in the air. But when I said that about a younger sister, he didn't understand... [*wrings her hands*] It's so awful I'm so plain. I am, I know I am. I heard people talking about me last Sunday, as we came out of church. One of the women said—[*Welsh accent*] —'She's a good girl, very kind-hearted. Shame about her looks.' [*own voice*] Shame about her looks!

       [HELEN *comes in. She goes to the window and opens it.*]

HELEN Storm's over. Lovely fresh air. Listen to the sea. [*Pause.*] Where's Dr Lloyd?

SIAN He's gone.

       [*Pause.*]

HELEN Sian...

SIAN Mmm?

HELEN How much longer are you going to go on being cross with me? We've not done each other any harm, have we? Why are we behaving like enemies? Isn't it time we made up?

       [SIAN *embraces her.*]

SIAN   Oh, I've wanted to, so much! All forgotten and forgiven?

HELEN   All forgotten and forgiven.

         [*Both are feeling very emotional.*]

SIAN   Has Dada gone to bed?

HELEN   No, he's in the sitting room. You and I haven't spoken properly for weeks, I really don't know why. [*sees the sideboard open*] What's been going on here?

SIAN   Dr Lloyd had some supper.

HELEN   Oh, look, and there's some wine left. Let's drink to our new friendship.

SIAN   All right.

HELEN   From the same glass. [*pours wine*] There!

         [*They drink and kiss.*]

         Now we're real friends.

SIAN   I've wanted it for so long, but I felt—I don't know, I was ashamed somehow...

         [*She starts to cry.*]

HELEN   Why are you crying?

SIAN   I don't know. I can't help it.

HELEN   There, there, now... [*starts crying herself*] You are silly. Now you've set me off. [*blows her nose*] You were angry because you thought I married your father for the wrong reasons. But I promise, I swear, I married him for love. He was a famous, clever person—I was bowled over. It may not have been true love—it may have only been an illusion —but it seemed true enough at the time. I didn't marry him for money. But from the very day of our wedding you've looked at me sideways with your clever, suspicious eyes.

SIAN   Pax! Pax! We said all forgotten.

HELEN   You shouldn't look at people like that. It doesn't

suit you. You have to trust people, or life's impossible.

> [*Pause.*]

SIAN   Tell me—honestly—as a friend—are you happy?

HELEN   No.

SIAN   I knew you weren't. And—honestly again—would you have liked a younger husband?

HELEN   What a baby you are. Of course I would. [*laughs*] Go on, ask me something else. Go on.

SIAN   Do you like Dr Lloyd?

HELEN   Yes. Very much.

SIAN   Am I blushing? I am, aren't I? He's gone, but I can still hear his voice, his footsteps ... When I look out into the darkness, I see his face. I have to tell someone, but I daren't say it out loud, I'm too ashamed. Let's go to my room and talk there. Am I very silly? I am, aren't I? Tell me about him ...

HELEN   What can I tell you?

SIAN   He's clever—he can do anything he wants—he can cure people of their illnesses, he plants trees ...

HELEN   Oh, it's not just trees and pills, Sian dear. He's got real talent, I think. And to be talented, you have to have courage, you need an open mind, a bold imagination. He plants a tree, and sees at once what it'll be in a thousand years' time, he sees its effect on the future happiness of mankind. People like that are so rare—you *ought* to love him. Oh, he gets drunk now and then, he speaks coarsely—but so what? A man of talent's not a new-born babe. Think of his daily life. Terrible roads, farm-tracks, really, ruts, mud, long distances—rough, mean-spirited people—poverty and sickness everywhere. You can hardly expect someone who works night and day in conditions like that to be pure and sober

at almost forty years of age. [*kisses her*] I wish you
happiness with all my heart. You deserve it. [*gets
up*] As for me, I'm just a boring minor character—
in my music, my married life, my husband's house,
my flirtations—I've always been a minor character
all my life. When I come to think of it, Sian, I'm
really very, very unhappy. [*walks up and down in
agitation*] I shall never be happy on this earth.
Never. Why are you laughing?

SIAN [*hiding her face in her hands*] I'm so happy—so
happy.

HELEN I feel like music. Do you? Shall I play something?

SIAN Oh, yes, please. [*embraces her*] I shan't go to sleep
now. Please play.

HELEN Oh. But your father's still awake. And music
irritates him when he isn't feeling well. You go and
ask him—would he mind if I play? Go on.

SIAN All right.

[*She goes. The* GAMEKEEPER *is whistling for his
dogs.*]

HELEN It's so long since I played. It'll make me cry. I'll cry
like a baby. [*goes to the window*] Is that you,
Roberts?

ROBERTS [*off*] Yes, madam.

HELEN Pheasants all right? No poachers tonight?

ROBERTS [*off*] Not that I see, madam.

HELEN Well, don't whistle then. The master's not well.

ROBERTS [*off*] I was just going home, any road. [*calls*] Here,
boy! Here! Come by here!

[*Pause. Then* SIAN *returns.*]

SIAN He says no.

End of Act Two

Act Three

*The drawing room. Nearly one o'clock in the afternoon.
There are three doors: one to the right, one to the left,
one in the centre.*

*IEUAN and SIAN are sitting. HELEN is pacing up and
down, absorbed in her own thoughts.*

IEUAN   It would appear that Herr Professor Blathwaite has
expressed the wish for our assemblage here at one
o'clock. [*looks at his watch*] Quarter to. He means
to issue some statement to the world.

HELEN   It's probably business.

IEUAN   He has no business. All he does is write twaddle,
grumble and feel jealous.

SIAN   Uncle!

IEUAN   All right, all right, I'm sorry. [*looks at* HELEN] Look
at her. So lazy she can hardly stay upright as she
walks. [*ironic*] Very charming. Very charming indeed.

HELEN   What are you droning on about now? All you do is
drone. Don't you ever get tired of it? [*miserable*] I'm
so bored—I think I may die of boredom.

SIAN   [*shrugs*] If you want work, I can find you some.

HELEN   For instance?

SIAN   You could help on the farm. You could teach. Visit
the sick. There's plenty to do if you look. Before
you and Dada came, Uncle Ieuan and I used to go
to all the local sheep fairs—Penmorfa, Dolben-
maen, Criccieth—we went as far as Dolgellau.

HELEN   But I wouldn't know how to buy a sheep. Anyway,

I'm not interested. And it's only in novels that
people visit the sick. You can't expect me to
suddenly begin teaching and nursing.

SIAN   I really don't understand how you can not want to.
Give yourself time, you'll soon get used to the idea.
[*embraces her*] Don't be bored, love. [*laughs*] All this
boredom and idleness is infectious. Because you're
bored and don't know what to do, Uncle Ieuan does
nothing either, just follows you round like your
shadow. And here am I, I've stopped work to come
and chat to you—I've become lazy too, can't help
myself. As for Dr Lloyd—he never used to come
here more than once a month, and then only after
much persuasion. But now here he is, driving over
every day, neglecting his trees and his patients... I
think you're a witch.

IEUAN   Don't look so miserable, Helen. [*eager*] Come on,
you're such a gorgeous creature, pull yourself together. There's mermaid's blood in your veins—so
be a mermaid. Let yourself go. Fall head over heels
in love with a water sprite—plunge into the whirl-
pool. Then the Herr Professor and the rest of us
can throw up our hands in shock and horror.

HELEN   [*angry*] Leave me alone. You're so stupid!

        [*She starts to go but* IEUAN *stops her.*]

IEUAN   Now, now, my dear, I'm sorry—I apologise. [*kisses
her*] Pax?

HELEN   You'd try the patience of a saint.

IEUAN   In the interests of peace and harmony I'll go and
get you a bunch of roses. I got them ready for you
this morning—late summer roses—lovely, mournful
roses.

        [*He goes.*]

SIAN   Late summer roses—lovely, mournful roses ...

        [HELEN *and* SIAN *look out of the window.*]

HELEN   Nearly September already. How on earth will we get through the winter? [*Pause.*] Where *is* Dr Lloyd?

SIAN   In Uncle Ieuan's study. Writing something. I'm glad Uncle's gone—I need to talk to you.

HELEN   What about?

SIAN   What about!

> [*She leans her head against* HELEN's *shoulder.* HELEN *strokes her hair.*]

HELEN   Now, now—there, there ...

SIAN   I'm so plain.

HELEN   You have lovely hair.

SIAN   Oh please! [*looks at herself in a mirror*] That's what they always say about plain girls. 'Lovely eyes, lovely hair ...' I've been in love with him for six years now. I love him more than my own mother. I hear him every minute of the day. I feel the touch of his hand ... I keep looking towards the door, hoping he'll be there. And now—well, you see how I keep coming to talk to you about him. And he's here every day, but he doesn't look at me, doesn't even notice me—it's absolute torture. I've no hope any more, none whatsoever. [*in despair*] Dear God, give me strength—I've been praying all night ... Sometimes I go up to him and start a conversation, I look right in his eyes—I've no pride left, I can't control myself. Yesterday, I just couldn't stop myself, I told Uncle Ieuan how much I loved him—all the servants know—all the tenants ...

HELEN   But not the doctor himself.

SIAN   It's as though I wasn't here.

HELEN   [*musing*] He's a strange man ... I tell you what—let me talk to him. I'll be very careful, just drop a hint ... [*Pause.*] You can't go on like this, you know, not knowing where you stand. Let me talk to him.

[SIAN *nods.*]

All right. Either he loves you or he doesn't—we'll soon find out. Don't be embarrassed, my dear—don't worry—I'll be so tactful he won't even notice I've asked. What we want to know is 'yes' or 'no'. Right? [*Pause.*] If it's 'no', he really shouldn't keep coming here, should he?

[SIAN *nods.*]

It's easier if you don't see them. All right, let's not put it off, let's do it now. He was going to show me some kind of sketch maps ... Go and tell him I can see him now.

SIAN   [*very agitated*] You'll tell me the truth, won't you? The whole truth?

HELEN   Of course I will. It's always better to know it, whatever it is. Uncertainty is so—unsettling. Trust me, Sian.

SIAN   Yes—all right—I'll say you want to see his maps.

[*She starts to go but stops.*]

You don't think ...? Sometimes—if you don't know—at least you can hope ...

HELEN   What?

SIAN   Nothing.

[*She goes.*]

HELEN   There's nothing worse than knowing a secret and not being able to help. [*thinks*] Of course, it's quite obvious he's not in love with her, but that doesn't mean he shouldn't marry her. She is plain, but then he's getting on and she'd make a splendid wife for a country doctor. She's intelligent, she's kind, she's very moral ... But that's not the point, it's not the point. Poor girl! [*Pause.*] She's bored to tears, surrounded by blobs of barely animate jelly instead of human beings, nothing to listen to but the inanities of people who only know how to eat, drink and sleep—then suddenly a man turns up like no one she's ever met—handsome, intelligent, attractive, like the moon rising on a dark night... Who wouldn't fall for him? Who wouldn't get carried away? I think I'm a little carried away myself... I'm certainly bored when he's not here. Look at me, smiling at the very thought of him. Ieuan says I've mermaid's blood in my veins, why don't I let myself go for once? Well, perhaps I should. Fly away like a bird, away from all these dreary people with their dreary faces and their dreary conversation—forget they ever existed... But I'm too much of a coward. Too scared. I'd be tormented with guilt. Yet he comes here every day, and I know perfectly well why, and I feel so awful about it, I ought to go down on my knees to Sian and beg her forgiveness, burst into tears...

[LLOYD *comes in, carrying maps.*]

LLOYD Good morning. You asked to see my maps.

HELEN You promised to show me them yesterday. But only if you've got time, of course.

LLOYD Of course. Where were you born?

[*He spreads out the maps on a card-table,* HELEN *helping.*]

HELEN London.

LLOYD And where did you study?

HELEN At the Royal College of Music.

LLOYD Then I'm afraid this won't interest you.

HELEN Why not? I may not know much about country life, but I've read a lot.

LLOYD Well—I have my own desk here, you know. In

Ieuan's study. When I'm completely done in, keeling over with exhaustion, I drop everything and drive over here to amuse myself for an hour or two with these. Ieuan and Sian scratch away at the accounts, and I sit next to them at my desk and paint. It's warm and peaceful—the dog dreams in front of the fire. But it's not a pleasure I allow myself very often, once a month perhaps. [*points to a map*] This is a map of England and Wales five hundred years ago. The dark and light green are forests—cover half the area, you see. This red here, this is where there were wolves and martens. This represents fauna and flora. Eagles and kites. These are churches and chapels, farms, villages—all kinds of human settlement, as you can see—mills ... The blue represents cattle, sheep and horses—lots of horses, of course.

[*He spreads out another map.*]

This is two hundred and fifty years ago. Now, only a third is forest. The wolves have gone, but there are still a few martens, kites and eagles. The green is already much diminished. And so on and so forth.

[*He spreads out a third map.*]

This is today. Woodland here and there, but only in patches, no continuous forest, no martens, no eagles. It's a steady, unignorable process of degeneration. In another fifteen or twenty years it'll be all over. You'll say, it's civilisation, inevitable, the old life giving way to new. And I'd understand that if, as a result of the forest disappearing, people were becoming healthier, wealthier, less hypocritical. But they're not, nothing of the sort. There are the same slum cottages, the same squalor, same lack of transport, poverty, typhoid, diphtheria, tuberculosis. It's sheer destruction, a direct result of the ruthless struggle to survive. But it's also a result of mental laziness, ignorance and irresponsibility. When a man's cold, hungry and sick, his instinct is to grab what's nearest to alleviate his hunger and give him warmth, he won't think twice about it. To save what's left of his life, to save his children, he'll destroy everything in his path. Why should he care about tomorrow? So everything's been destroyed, and nothing's been put in its place. [*coldly*] Right, well, I can see you're not interested, so ...

HELEN I just don't understand anything about it.

LLOYD There's nothing to understand. You're just not interested.

HELEN To tell you the truth, I was thinking about something else. I'm sorry. I have to ask you one or two questions and I'm embarrassed—I don't know how to begin.

LLOYD Questions?

HELEN Just one or two. Nothing difficult. Shall we sit down?

       [*They sit.*]

It's about a certain young person. May I be frank? No beating about the bush? Can we talk then forget everything we've said?

LLOYD All right.

HELEN It's my stepdaughter, Sian. Do you like her?

LLOYD Yes. Well, I respect her.

HELEN Do you like her as a woman?

       [*Short pause.*]

LLOYD No.

HELEN Not much more, and it's over. Haven't you noticed anything?

LLOYD No.

[HELEN *takes his hand.*]

HELEN You're not in love with her, I can see that. But she's so unhappy. Try to understand. And don't come here any more.

LLOYD Oh, I'm too old for all that. I've too much to do. [*shrugs*] Where would I find the time?

[*He is embarrassed.*]

HELEN Ouf! What a very unpleasant conversation. I've been so nervous—like carrying a great weight—thank goodness it's over. Now it must be as though we've never spoken and—and then you must say goodbye. You're intelligent, you understand ... [*Pause.*] Now I'm blushing myself.

LLOYD If you'd said something even a month or two ago, I might have ... Now ... [*shrugs*] If she's unhappy, then of course ... But what's in this for you? This cross-questioning? [*looks into her eyes and wags his finger at her*] You little devil!

HELEN What? What do you mean?

LLOYD [*laughs*] Little devil! All right, Sian's unhappy, I accept that, but what are you up to? [*stops her answering, animated*] Don't come all innocent with me, you know why I keep coming here—why, and for whom. You know perfectly well, you little sparrowhawk, looking at me like that. But I'm too smart an old sparrow for you.

HELEN What are you talking about? Sparrowhawk?

LLOYD A beautiful, preening polecat, if you'd rather—so long as you catch your prey. Well, I've done nothing for a whole month, given up all attempt at work, just to pursue you. And you've enjoyed it, enjoyed it immensely. What do you want me to say? I'm yours, you knew that without all these questions. [*raises his arms in surrender*] I surrender! Devour me!

HELEN .You're crazy!

LLOYD [*with a sardonic laugh*] Don't tell me you're not hungry?

HELEN I'm not like that at all, I— I promise you I never ...

    [*She starts to leave.*]

LLOYD [*stopping her*] I'll leave today, and I won't come back. But ... [*takes her hand, looks quickly round*] Where can we meet? Say—wherever you like. Quick—someone'll come. [*passionate*] You wonderful, gorgeous animal. Give me a kiss—let me at least kiss your beautiful scented hair ...

HELEN I swear to you...

LLOYD [*stopping her again*] Don't swear, no need to swear. No need for words at all. God, you're beautiful! Your hands!

    [*He kisses her hands.*]

HELEN Will you stop it! Please. Go away. [*gets her hands away*] You're completely forgetting yourself.

LLOYD All right, where can we meet tomorrow? [*puts his arm round her waist*] We're going to see each other, it's in the stars.

    [*As he kisses her,* IEUAN *comes in with a bunch of roses, and stops in the doorway.* HELEN *fails to see him.*]

HELEN No ... No, leave me alone ...

    [*But she lays her head a moment on* LLOYD's *chest.*]

    No!

    [*She pulls away, but* LLOYD *keeps hold of her, his arm still round her waist.*]

LLOYD Come to the plantation tomorrow—two o'clock. All right? Will you be there? Say you'll be there.

    [*Now* HELEN *sees* IEUAN.]

HELEN   Let me go! This is awful!

> [*Deeply embarrassed, she goes towards the window.* IEUAN, *agitated, puts the roses on a chair, then wipes his face and neck with his handkerchief.*]

IEUAN   It's perfectly all right—really—perfectly...

LLOYD   [*with bravado*] Turned out fine after all, didn't it, Ieuan? Very overcast this morning, looked like rain, but the sun's out now. In fact, it's a lovely August. The winter oats are looking really good. [*rolls up the maps*] Pity the days are getting shorter.

> [*He goes.* HELEN *goes quickly to* IEUAN.]

HELEN   Ieuan, will you please, please, do everything you can to make sure my husband and I leave here today. Do you understand? Today!

IEUAN   [*wiping his face*] What? Well, yes—all right. I saw it all, Helen. Everything.

HELEN   [*nervous*] Did you hear what I said? I must leave this place today.

> [BLATHWAITE, SIAN, PROSSER *and* GWEN *come in.*]

PROSSER   As a matter of fact, Professor, I haven't been feeling too well myself the last day or two. Something not quite right up here...

BLATHWAITE   Where is everyone? I can't stand this house, it's a perfect labyrinth. Twenty-six enormous rooms, people wandering off in all directions—you can never find anyone you want. Sian—ask your grandmother and Helen to come here, please.

HELEN   I am here.

BLATHWAITE   Well—shall we all be seated then?

> [SIAN *goes up to* HELEN, *impatient to know.*]

SIAN   What did he say?

HELEN   Later.

SIAN   You're trembling. You're upset. [*looks her in the eyes*] I see. He said he wouldn't be coming here again. Am I right? [*Pause.*] Please—I am right?

          [HELEN *nods.*]

BLATHWAITE [*to* PROSSER] I don't mind ill health, that's inevitable, it's Welsh country life I can't stick. I feel I've fallen off the earth and landed on some undiscovered planet. Will everyone please be seated ... Sian!

          [SIAN *doesn't hear him. She is in misery, standing with hanging head.*]

          Sian!

          [*No effect.*]

          She's not listening. Gwen, you may sit.

          [GWEN *sits and starts knitting.*]

          Now, ladies and gentlemen, I'm asking you all to, as the phrase goes, lend me your ears.

IEUAN   [*agitated*] Look, you don't need me—please may I go?

BLATHWAITE No, you may not. I need you more than anyone.

IEUAN   What can you possibly need me for?

BLATHWAITE Don't snap at me. [*Pause, then formally*] I'm sorry. If I've upset you in any way, please accept my apologies.

IEUAN   Oh, for God's sake! Get on with it, whatever it is.

          [MAIR *enters.*]

BLATHWAITE Ah, here's Mother. So, ladies and gentlemen—shall we begin? [*Pause.*] I've brought you all together to tell you that we're about to have a visit from the Welsh Land Commission. [*Not a titter.*] Joking apart, we have a serious matter to discuss. I've brought you together because I need your help and advice. Knowing how willing you've been to offer guidance in the past, I'm sure I can count on it today. I'm an intellectual, a literary sort of chap, I've never been very good at the practical side of life. And I can't manage without the advice of those of you who are—Ieuan, and Mr Prosser, you, Mother ... The fact is—'manet omnes una nox'. We are all in God's hands, and I am old and ill. It's time, therefore, to put my affairs in order, particularly in so far as they concern my family. I'm not thinking of myself—my day is done. But I have a young wife, and an unmarried daughter.

[*Pause.*]

I simply cannot go on living in Wales. My wife and I are just not made for the life. However—we can't live in London either, not on the income from this estate. We could, of course, sell off our woods, but that would be a once-for-all measure, not one we could repeat. We need, therefore, to find some way of guaranteeing a permanent, more or less definite income. I've thought long and hard about the matter, and this is the solution I offer for your consideration. You don't want the details, I'll just give you a general outline. On average, this estate yields two per cent per annum. I propose we sell it. If the money were re-invested in securities, we could expect four or five per cent, and there might even be something over to buy a country cottage in Sussex or Kent.

IEUAN Hold on, hold on—I don't think I can have heard correctly. Would you mind repeating what you just said?

BLATHWAITE We invest the money in securities, live in London and buy a country cottage with the surplus.

IEUAN Not the country cottage—before that.

BLATHWAITE I propose we should sell the estate.

IEUAN   Oh, you *did* say that! You sell the estate. First class, wonderful idea. And what do you propose to do with me? And my mother? And with Sian here?

BLATHWAITE   There's plenty of time to discuss all that. We can't decide everything at once.

IEUAN   Sorry, but ... I've been extremely stupid. Obviously. So stupid, I thought the estate belonged to Sian. My father bought it as a dowry for my sister. And all these years I've been naive enough to believe that my sister's estate had gone to her daughter.

BLATHWAITE   The estate does, indeed, belong to Sian. No one disputes that. And I couldn't take the decision to sell it without her consent. But what I'm proposing is in fact in Sian's interest.

IEUAN   But that's impossible. Unbelievable! Either that or I've finally gone mad.

MAIR   Ieuan, don't contradict Alexander. I'm sure he knows best.

IEUAN   He most certainly does not. May I have a glass of water? [*drinks*] All right, go on, say what you want to say, whatever it is.

BLATHWAITE   I don't see why you're so upset. I don't pretend my solution is ideal, and if you all disagree with it, I shall not, of course, insist.

[*Pause.*]

PROSSER   [*embarrassed*] You know how much I respect education, Professor—it's in the blood you might say. My brother's wife's brother, Haydn Price, Caergybi—you've probably heard of him—he's a BA Cardiff, you know—he ...

IEUAN   Pocky, for God's sake—later! We're trying to talk business. [*to* BLATHWAITE] Ask Pocky. We bought the estate from his uncle.

BLATHWAITE   There's no point in going into all that.

IEUAN   Nineteen thousand five hundred pounds my father paid. Well, he only paid seventeen, actually, two thousand five hundred was on mortgage. But you listen here—he'd never have bought it at all if I hadn't given up my share of the inheritance in favour of my sister Hannah. Whom I loved very dearly. And you'll kindly recall that I worked like a slave for ten years, while the rents were falling, to pay the mortgage off.

BLATHWAITE   I'm sorry I ever started this conversation.

IEUAN   It's entirely due to me that this estate is currently free of debt and in good condition. And now I'm old you want to throw me out by the scruff of my neck.

BLATHWAITE   What are you trying to say?

IEUAN   What I'm trying to say is, I've run this place for twenty-five years, worked hard, sent you money like the most conscientious bailiff you could hope to employ, and in all that time you've never once said thank you. In all that time—from start to finish— you've allowed me fifty pounds a year—pathetic! You've never given me a single rise!

BLATHWAITE   But, Ieuan, I didn't know. I'm not a practical man, I don't understand these things. You could have given yourself a rise.

IEUAN   Oh, that's a great idea. I could have been a thief, you mean. I suppose you all despise me for not being a thief. It would have been perfectly fair, and I wouldn't be a pauper now.

MAIR   Ieuan!

PROSSER   [upset] Ieuan, old fellow, don't, please don't... You're upsetting everybody. Don't let's spoil old friendships. [pats him on the shoulder] That's enough, now.

IEUAN   For twenty-five years my mother and I have sat

within these four walls like a pair of moles ... We've thought and dreamed about you the whole time, no one else—nothing. We've talked about you all day long, about your work, we've been so proud of you. We've never uttered your name without singing its praises. And all night long we've ruined our eyesight reading books and articles for which I now have nothing but contempt.

PROSSER Ieuan, don't—please—I beg you ...

BLATHWAITE [*angry*] Will you please just tell me what you want?

IEUAN You were in a higher sphere than us. We learned your articles by heart. But now—now I can see. See right through you. You write about art, but you don't understand the first thing about it. All the work we admired is trash. You've cheated us!

BLATHWAITE For God's sake ... Calm him down, someone. I'm going.

HELEN Ieuan, stop it! Stop it at once. Do you hear me?

IEUAN No, I won't stop it!

[*He bars* BLATHWAITE's *way.*]

Not till I've finished. You've ruined my life—I haven't had a life. I haven't lived. I've wasted and ruined the best years of my life, entirely because of you. You're the worst enemy I ever had.

PROSSER I can't stand this—I can't take it—I'm off ...

[*He leaves, very upset.*]

BLATHWAITE But what do you *want*? And what right have you got to talk to me like this? You're pathetic. If the estate's yours, take it. I don't want it.

HELEN This is hell. I'm going. [*shouts*] I can't stand any more.

IEUAN I might as well be dead. I was an able, clever, stout-hearted sort of fellow ... If I'd had a normal life, I might have been a Schopenhauer, a Dosto-

evsky, a John Stuart Mill, a Charles Dickens ...
What am I talking about? I'm going mad ... Mother,
I'm so unhappy—Mother!

MAIR Just do what Alexander says.

[SIAN *kneels beside* GWEN.]

SIAN Oh, Gwenny, Gwenny cariad!

IEUAN Mother! What shall I do? No, you don't have to tell
me. I know. [*to* BLATHWAITE] You're not going to
forget me!

[*He goes out through the centre door.* MAIR
follows him.]

BLATHWAITE Why do I have to put up with this? He's mad. Can't
someone get rid of him? I won't stay under the
same roof. [*points to the door through which* IEUAN
has gone] He'll have to move to a cottage, or the
north wing. Or I'll move. But I simply will not
remain in the same house.

HELEN [*to* BLATHWAITE] We're leaving. Tonight. You must
make the arrangements at once.

BLATHWAITE Pathetic man.

[SIAN *is still on her knees.*]

SIAN [*to* BLATHWAITE, *agitated, through tears*] Try to be
kind, Dada. Uncle Ieuan and I are so unhappy.
[*being brave*] Try and understand. Years ago, Uncle
Ieuan and Grandmama sat up night after night,
reading your books, copying out your manuscripts,
night after night. And Uncle Ieuan and I, we've
never had a holiday, we've never spent a penny on
ourselves, we've sent everything to you ... We've
earned our keep, really we have. I'm not saying it
well, Dada, but you must try and understand.

HELEN [*agitated*] Alexander, for God's sake, go and talk to
him—please.

BLATHWAITE Well, all right, I'll try. It's not as though I've accused him of anything. I'm not angry with him. But you must admit his behaviour—well, it's bizarre, to say the least. But I'll see what I can do.

[*He goes through the centre door.*]

HELEN Be nice to him—try and calm him down.

[*She goes with* BLATHWAITE. SIAN *clings to* GWEN.]

SIAN Gwenny, Gwenny cariad ...

GWEN Don't you pay any attention, Sianny. Ganders hiss and cocks cackle, but they soon stop, they soon stop.

SIAN Gwenny!

GWEN [*stroking her head*] You're cold, your teeth are chattering. There, there, 'y ngeneth Annwyl i— God'll look after you. A nice cup of tea, and you'll soon feel better. Don't fret yourself, 'y ngeneth bach amddifad i.

[*She looks at the centre door.*]

[*with feeling*] What a din they do make, those ganders. Damn them!

[*There is a shot off-stage, then a shriek from* HELEN. SIAN *jumps up, startled.*]

Curse and damn them!

[BLATHWAITE *comes rushing in, terrified.*]

BLATHWAITE Stop him! For God's sake, someone stop him. He's raving mad!

[HELEN *and* IEUAN *are struggling in the door-way.* IEUAN *has a 12-bore shotgun.*]

HELEN Give that here! Give it to me, I said!

IEUAN Let me go! Helen, if you don't let me go...

[*He frees himself from* HELEN *and comes search-ing for* BLATHWAITE.]

Where is he? There!

[*He shoots.*]

Bang! Missed him. Failed again. Lord God of Sabaoth!

> [*He flings the gun on the floor and sinks into a chair.* BLATHWAITE *is shattered.* HELEN *leans against the wall to stop herself fainting.*]

HELEN   Get me out of here. Take me away, kill me—anything, so long as I don't have to stay here.

IEUAN   [*in despair*] What am I doing? What am I doing?

SIAN   [*softly*] Gwenny! Gwenny—cariad!

End of Act Three

Act Four

IEUAN's room. Evening.

*IEUAN's room is both his personal room and the office
from which the estate is run. There is a large table by
the window, covered with ledgers and papers, a desk, a
cupboard, a pair of scales. There is also a smaller table
for LLOYD, with drawing materials, paints, and a
drawing board. There is a bird cage with a starling in
it. There is a large map of Africa on the wall. There is
a large sofa covered in imitation leather. To the left a
door leads to IEUAN's bedroom; to the right another
leads to the hall. In front of the latter there is a
doormat for the boots of the tenants coming to see
IEUAN.*

*It is quiet. PROSSER and GWEN are sitting facing each
other, winding wool.*

PROSSER Come on, Gwenny, for goodness' sake. They'll be
wanting to say goodbye in a minute. They've or-
dered the carriage.

GWEN [*speeding up*] Nearly done.

PROSSER Going to Cheltenham. Going to live in Cheltenham!

GWEN And a good thing too.

PROSSER Had the fright of their lives, they have. 'I'm not
staying here,' says Mrs Blathwaite. 'Not a moment
longer, I'm not. We've got to go,' she says, 'Right
away. We'll go to Cheltenham, look around for
somewhere, send for the luggage after.' Not taking
much with them, Gwenny. They weren't meant to
live here, that's what it is, just not meant to live
here.

GWEN   Can't say I'm sorry. All that noise last night, and as for the shooting ... I don't know, I really don't.

PROSSER   Someone should put it in a book. Henty. G.A. Henty. He could do it justice.

GWEN   I wouldn't want to read it. [*Pause.*] Well, any road, now we can go back to the way things were. Breakfast at eight, dinner at one, supper in the evening. Everything in the right place at the right time, like proper Christians. [*sighs*] It's a shame, it's that long since I had a nice bowl of cawl.

PROSSER   Yes, haven't had cawl for ages. [*Pause.*] Not for a long time. You know what happened this morning, Gwenny? I was walking down the village, minding my own business, when Hugh Price, baker, his son Gwynfor, he shouted at me. 'There goes the sponger!' he said. Sponger, he called me. I was most upset.

GWEN   Pay no attention to it, 'y ngwas aur i. We all sponge on God. You and Sian and Ieuan—we're all the same. We don't sit around doing nothing, do we? We all work, work hard. Where is Sian?

PROSSER   In the garden. She and the doctor, they're looking for Ieuan. Afraid he might do himself a damage.

GWEN   Where's the gun?

PROSSER   [*whispers*] Hid it in the cellar.

GWEN   Duw a'n gwaredo, what a carry-on!

[IEUAN *and* LLOYD *come in by the outside door.*]

IEUAN   Leave me alone! [*to* GWEN *and* PROSSER] Go away, please. Leave me alone—just for an hour. I can't bear it, the way you all watch me.

PROSSER   On my way, Ieuan.

[*He tiptoes off.*]

GWEN   Hiss, hiss, hiss goes the gander!

[*She goes off, taking her knitting.*]

IEUAN Will you please leave me alone!

LLOYD Gladly. In fact I can't wait. But I can't go till you give me back what you took.

IEUAN I didn't take anything.

LLOYD Come on. Don't waste any more of my time. I should have been gone hours ago.

IEUAN I didn't take anything.

[*They both sit.*]

LLOYD Of course not. Well, all right, I'll wait a little longer, but then, I'm afraid, I shall have to use force. I'll tie you up and search you. I'm serious, Ieuan.

IEUAN Do what you want. [*Pause.*] How can I have made such a fool of myself? Fired twice and missed both times. I'll never forgive myself.

LLOYD If you must shoot someone, why not shoot yourself?

IEUAN [*shrugs*] It's very odd. I've tried to commit a murder, but no one's had me arrested. I haven't been charged. Which means they must all think I'm mad. [*bitter laugh*] Me, mad! When people whose mediocrity, and stupidity, and total lack of feeling is hidden under the cloak of that learned oracle, a professor—they're not mad, oh, no, not at all. And people who marry old men, and then deceive them in front of the whole neighbourhood, they're not mad, either. I saw you. I saw you kiss her.

LLOYD Yes. I kissed her. [*blows a raspberry*] So what?

IEUAN [*glances towards the door*] What *is* mad is the world out there, letting people like you in.

LLOYD That's just stupid.

IEUAN But I'm mad. Irresponsible. I'm allowed to be stupid.

LLOYD   Very clever. Only you're not mad, just a little touched. A 'character'. I used to think mad people were ill—abnormal. But I've decided it's perfectly normal to be a little touched. So you're normal.

IEUAN   [*covers his face with his hands*] I'm so ashamed. If you knew how ashamed I was. The sting of shame—there's nothing like it. [*sad*] It's unbearable. [*leans across the table*] What shall I do? What shall I do?

LLOYD   Nothing.

IEUAN   Give me something, for God's sake! I'm forty-seven, I may live to be sixty, that's another thirteen years. Eternity! How am I going to live through another thirteen years? What am I going to do? How am I going to get through the days? You see ... [*clasps* LLOYD's *hand eagerly*] You see, if we could just live the rest of our lives differently, somehow ... If I could wake up one fine morning and feel I was starting my life all over again, that the past was forgotten, blown away like smoke ... [*weeps*] How can I do it? Tell me. How can I start again?

LLOYD   [*sad*] Come on ... No one can do that. How could they? You and I—our lives are hopeless.

IEUAN   Do you really think so?

LLOYD   Yes.

IEUAN   Then give me something. [*points to his chest*] In here, it's like a furnace ...

LLOYD   [*loud, angry*] Stop it, Ieuan. [*gentle*] A hundred, two hundred years from now, people'll despise us for the stupid, thoughtless way we carry on—they'll have found the secret of happiness, perhaps. But there's only one thing for us to look forward to. The chance that when we're safely tucked up in our coffins, we may have the occasional, pleasant dream. [*sighs*] You know, in this whole county there were only ever two decent, intelligent people—you

and me. But after ten years of this narrow-minded,
contemptible little world, we've gone downhill.
Now we're as contemptible as the rest. Our blood's
been poisoned by their putrid attitudes. We've
become as vulgar and dreary as they are. [*quick*]
That's enough of that. Give me back what you took.

IEUAN Didn't take anything.

LLOYD You took a bottle of morphine from my bag.
[*Pause.*] Look, if you're absolutely determined to do
yourself in, go and shoot yourself in the woods. But
first give me back my morphine, or there'll be
gossip and speculation and people will say I gave it
to you. Come on, it's bad enough I'll have to do
your post-mortem. You think that's an amusing
prospect?

[SIAN *comes in.*]

IEUAN Leave me alone.

LLOYD Sian, your uncle's taken a bottle of morphine from
my bag and he won't give it back. Would you tell
him it's really not very clever. And I'm pressed for
time. I ought to be on my way.

SIAN Uncle, did you take the morphine?

[*Pause.*]

LLOYD Of course he did. I know he did.

SIAN Give it back. Why are you trying to frighten us?
[*gentle*] Please, Uncle. I'm just as unhappy as you
are, but I'm not giving in. I'm keeping going, I'm
going to keep going till my dying day. And so must
you. [*Pause.*] Uncle! Please! [*kisses him*] Uncle,
darling, dearest Uncle, give it back. [*weeps*] Be
kind, think about us, hand it back. Endurance,
Uncle! Endurance!

[IEUAN *takes the bottle from the drawer of the
table and hands it to* LLOYD.]

IEUAN   All right, here you are. [*to* SIAN] But we must do
        something, get back to work, at once, or I won't—I
        shan't be able to ...

  SIAN Yes, of course—work. As soon as we've seen them
        off, we'll get right down to it. [*arranges papers with
        nervous fingers*] We've let everything go to rack and
        ruin ...

              [LLOYD *puts the bottle in his bag and straps it
              up.*]

LLOYD   Right, then, I'll be off.

              [HELEN *comes in.*]

HELEN   Oh, Ieuan, you're here. We're just leaving, but ...
        Would you have a word with Alexander? There's
        something he wants to say to you.

  SIAN Come on, Uncle.

              [*She takes him by the arm.*]

        We'll go together. You and Dada must make it up.
        You really must.

              [SIAN *and* IEUAN *go.*]

HELEN   We're off. [*offers her hand to* LLOYD] Goodbye.

LLOYD   Already?

HELEN   The carriage is at the door.

LLOYD   Goodbye, then.

HELEN   You promised me you'd leave today yourself.

LLOYD   On my way. [*Pause.*] Were you frightened? [*takes
        her hand*] Was it really so alarming?

HELEN   Yes.

LLOYD   But if you stayed ... Mmm? Tomorrow at the plan-
        tation ...?

HELEN   No. It's all settled. And if we hadn't decided to go,
        I couldn't look you in the face. But there's one
        thing I want you to do for me. I want you to try to

think the best of me. Try to feel some respect for
me.

LLOYD [*impatient*] Oh, for God's sake, stay! Face up to it.
You've got nothing whatever to do, no purpose in
life, nothing to fill your time—sooner or later you're
bound to let yourself go—it's inevitable. Isn't it
better to do it here, out in the open, instead of
Cheltenham or Bath? It's poetic here, at least, it's a
beautiful season—there are woods and trees,
crumbling country houses...

HELEN Very amusing. Though I'm angry with you now, I
shall remember you with pleasure. You're an interesting, original man. And as we'll never meet
again—I may as well say it—I was a little in love
with you. But now—let's shake hands and part
friends. And do try to think of me kindly.

LLOYD [*shakes her hand*] All right, off you go. [*thoughtful*]
You seem like a good, decent person. But there's
something strange about you. As soon as you and
your husband arrived, everyone who'd been so
busy, beavering away out here to try and get
something done—everyone dropped whatever he
was doing and devoted the entire summer to you
and your husband's gout. The pair of you infected
us all with your idleness. Look at me. I've done
nothing for the last month, while people have been
sick and—and the farmers have let their cattle
graze in my woods, on my young trees... Wherever
you and the Professor go you carry destruction with
you. I'm joking, of course, but... It's very odd, but
I'm quite sure if you'd stayed any longer, the
devastation would have been complete. I'd have
been destroyed, for one. And as for you—you
wouldn't have got off scot free, either. Well, off you
go. Finita la Commedia!

[HELEN *takes a pencil from his table and hides it away.*]

HELEN I'm taking this pencil to remember you by.

LLOYD It's funny. We've just got to know one another, and now, for the stupidest reasons, we'll never see each other again. The whole world's like that. Look, while we're alone—before Ieuan comes back with another bunch of flowers—may I—kiss you? A farewell kiss—yes? [*kisses her on the cheek*] There. All over.

HELEN I wish you every happiness. [*looks round*] And for once in my life—here goes!

[*She kisses him suddenly; they both quickly withdraw.*]

I must go.

LLOYD Yes. Quickly. If the carriage is there ...

HELEN Someone's coming.

[*They both listen.*]

LLOYD Finita!

[BLATHWAITE *comes in with* IEUAN, MAIR *(with a book)*, PROSSER *and* SIAN.]

BLATHWAITE So! Let bygones be bygones. After all that's occurred, all that I've lived through and pondered on these last few hours, I'm ready to write something for posterity—a whole thesis on 'Life as it should be lived'. I accept your apologies wholeheartedly and beg you to accept mine. Goodbye.

[*He and* IEUAN *shake hands formally.*]

IEUAN You'll be getting the same regular payments as before. Everything will be just as it was.

[HELEN *kisses* SIAN.]

BLATHWAITE Mother...

[*He kisses* MAIR.]

MAIR   [*returning the kiss*] Have a new photograph taken, Alexander, and send me a copy. You know how dear you are to me.

PROSSER   Goodbye, Professor. Don't forget us.

BLATHWAITE   [*kissing* SIAN] Goodbye—goodbye, all.

[*He shakes hands with* LLOYD, *then addresses the whole group.*]

Thank you for your good company. I admire your way of thinking, your generous spirit, your enthusiasm. But allow an old man to add one word as he says goodbye. You must get down to work. Contribute to society! [*waving round*] Goodbye. Goodbye.

[*He goes, with* SIAN *and* MAIR.]

IEUAN   [*kissing* HELEN *warmly*] Goodbye—please forgive me—we shan't see each other again.

HELEN   Goodbye, my dear.

[*She kisses the top of his head, and goes.*]

LLOYD   [*to* PROSSER] Pocky, tell them to bring up my trap, would you?

PROSSER   Of course, my dear fellow.

[*He goes, leaving* LLOYD *and* IEUAN *alone.* LLOYD *clears the painting things off his table and puts them in a case.*]

LLOYD   Aren't you going to see them off?

IEUAN   No, no—let them go, I—it's too painful. I must do something—now! Work—get to work!

[*He starts going through the papers on his desk. Pause. Then we hear the sound of the carriage driving off.*]

LLOYD   They've gone. I bet the Professor's relieved. We shan't be seeing him here again.

[GWEN *comes in.*]

GWEN   They've gone.

        [GWEN sits and starts knitting. SIAN comes in.]

SIAN   They've gone. *[wipes her eyes]* God bless them. *[to IEUAN]* That's right, Uncle, let's get down to it.

IEUAN   Work, work...

SIAN   It's so long since we sat down together at this table.

        [She lights the lamp.]

    No ink.

        [She goes to the cupboard and fills the inkstand.]

    I'm sorry they've gone.

        [MAIR enters slowly.]

MAIR   They've gone.

        [She sits down and buries herself in her book. SIAN sits at the table and opens a ledger.]

SIAN   We could start by making out the bills, Uncle. We've fallen so far behind. Mr Jones was asking for his account only this morning. Edwin Jones. Pick up your pen. You do one, I'll do another.

IEUAN   On account to—Mr Edwin Jones...

        [They write in silence.]

GWEN   I'm ready for beddy-byes.

LLOYD   It's so quiet. Pens scratching, sheep baa-ing. So warm and cosy. I don't want to go.

        [The sound of a pony and trap.]

    My trap. Well. That's it. Nothing more to do except say goodbye to you all. Goodbye to my table. And off I go.

        [He puts the maps into their portfolio.]

GWEN   Don't go hurrying off now. Sit down a bit.

LLOYD   No. Mustn't.

IEUAN   *[writing]* On account to... Two pounds, fifteen shillings...

[*A* SERVANT *enters.*]

SERVANT Your trap's at the door, Doctor.

LLOYD I heard.

[*He hands his bags and the portfolio to the* SERVANT.]

Put these in, would you? Mind you don't bend the portfolio.

SERVANT Very good, sir.

[*The* SERVANT *goes.*]

LLOYD Well...

[*He moves towards the others to say goodbye.*]

SIAN When will we see you again?

LLOYD Oh, not for a long time, I shouldn't think. Probably not this winter. Of course, if there's anything wrong, you let me know, and I'll come at once. [*shakes her hand*] Thank you for all the meals I've eaten, your hospitality, your great kindness—thank you for everything.

[*He kisses* GWEN *on the top of her head.*]

Yn iach, Gwenny.

GWEN Iechyd da, 'y nghariad i. You're not going without your tea?

LLOYD I don't really want any, thanks.

GWEN What about a drop of whisky, then?

LLOYD [*unsure*] Well, but—perhaps.

[GWEN *goes off. Pause.*]

My horse is going lame. I noticed yesterday when Evans was watering him.

IEUAN Have to get her reshod.

LLOYD I'll call in at the blacksmith at Penrhyndeudraeth. Never mind.

[*He goes and looks at the map of Africa.*]

Must be terrific out there—the heat—scorching, it must be, in Africa. Terrible.

IEUAN   Very probably.

> [GWEN *returns with a tray with a glass of whisky and a sandwich.*]

GWEN   Here you are, then.

> [LLOYD *swallows the whisky at a gulp.*]

Iechyd da! But eat your sandwich.

LLOYD   No, I prefer the whisky on its own. Well—all the best. [*to* GWEN] Don't bother to see me off. No need.

> [*He goes.* SIAN *follows with a candle.* GWEN *resumes her seat.*]

IEUAN   [*writing*] February 2nd—hay—one ton. February 16th, two tons. Straw...

> [*The sound of the pony and trap going away.*]

GWEN   He's gone.

> [*Pause.* SIAN *returns and puts the candle back on the table.*]

SIAN   He's gone.

IEUAN   [*counting on his fingers*] Total—fifteen shillings—one pound, seven and sixpence...

> [SIAN *sits and begins to write.* GWEN *yawns.*]

GWEN   Duw a faddeuo'n pechode ni! Mercy on us...

> [PROSSER *enters on tiptoe, sits near the door, and takes out his mouth organ.*]

IEUAN   [*to* SIAN] Sian—I'm so unhappy. If only you knew how unhappy I am.

SIAN   There's nothing to be done, Uncle, we must just go on. [*Pause.*] And we shall. We shall go on through a long, long, succession of days, with even longer evenings. We'll suffer with patience the tribulations that fate sends. We'll work for others, on into old age. We shall know no rest. When our time comes, we shall die, resigned to our fate. And then, beyond the grave, we shall tell of our suffering, how we wept, all the troubles we endured. God will have pity on us, and you and I, dear Uncle Ieuan, we'll know a life of brightness, beauty and splendour. We'll rejoice, and look back on this unhappiness with affection, with a smile, almost. And we shall find peace. I believe that, Uncle, I believe it with all my heart and soul.

[*She kneels in front of him and lays her head in his hands. Her voice is tired.*]

We shall find peace.

[PROSSER *quietly plays his mouth organ. We hear, too, the distant waves on the shore.*]

We shall find peace. We'll hear the angels, we'll see the whole sky studded with diamonds, and all the evil of the world, and all our suffering, will be washed away by the grace which will cover the whole earth, and our life will be peaceful, gentle, sweet as kisses. I believe that—I really do.

[*She wipes the tears from his eyes.*]

Poor Uncle, poor Uncle Ieuan, you're crying ... [*through her own tears*] You've never known happiness in this life, but wait, Uncle, wait—we shall find peace.

[*We hear the* GAMEKEEPER *calling his dogs.* PROSSER *plays.* MAIR *makes a note on her book.* GWEN *knits. The sound of the sea grows louder.*]

We shall find peace.

The End.